LIN-MANUEL MIRANDA
Making a Difference as a Writer

By Katie Kawa

KidHaven PUBLISHING

People Who Make a Difference

Published in 2021 by
KidHaven Publishing, an Imprint of Greenhaven Publishing, LLC
353 3rd Avenue
Suite 255
New York, NY 10010

Designer: Deanna Paternostro
Editor: Katie Kawa

Photo credits: Cover, p. 15 Gladys Vega/Getty Images Entertainment/Getty Images; p. 5 lev radin/Shutterstock.com; pp. 7, 11, Walter McBride/WireImage/Getty Images; p. 9 Theo Wargo/ WireImage/Getty Images; p. 13 Walter McBride/Getty Images Entertainment/Getty Images; p. 17 (main) Kathy Hutchins/Shutterstock.com; p. 17 (inset) Katherine Frey/The Washington Post via Getty Images; p. 18 Tinseltown/Shutterstock.com; p. 20 Chip Somodevilla/Getty Images News/Getty Images; p. 21 T.Sumaetho/Shutterstock.com.

Cataloging-in-Publication Data

Names: Kawa, Katie.
Title: Lin-Manuel Miranda: making a difference as a writer / Katie Kawa.
Description: New York : KidHaven Publishing, 2021. | Series: People who make a difference | Includes glossary and index.
Identifiers: ISBN 9781534534643 (pbk.) | ISBN 9781534534667 (library bound) | ISBN 9781534534650 (6 pack) | ISBN 9781534534674 (ebook)
Subjects: LCSH: Miranda, Lin-Manuel, 1980—Juvenile literature. | Actors–United States–Biography–Juvenile literature.| Composers–United States–Biography–Juvenile literature.| Lyricists–United States--Biography–Juvenile literature.
Classification: LCC ML3930.M644 2021 | DDC 782.1'4092 B—dc23

Printed in the United States of America

CPSIA compliance information: Batch #BS20K: For further information contact Greenhaven Publishing LLC, New York, New York at 1-844-317-7404.

Please visit our website, www.greenhavenpublishing.com. For a free color catalog of all our high-quality books, call toll free 1-844-317-7404 or fax 1-844-317-7405.

Find us on

CONTENTS

A TALENTED STORYTELLER

Lin-Manuel Miranda is a man of many talents. He can act, he can sing, and he can rap. He's been in movies, on TV shows, and in Broadway **musicals**. However, he's perhaps best known as a writer. He's written musicals such as *In the Heights* and *Hamilton*, he's written songs for movies such as *Moana*, and his writing on **social media** has been turned into a book.

Lin-Manuel Miranda's words have **inspired** many people. He's made the world a better place by telling stories that make everyone feel included. He's shown that writers can make a big difference in the world around them!

In His Words

"I believe your **responsibility** as a storyteller, especially in the theater, is to give people the time of their lives and tell a great story well."

— Interview for the Nieman Foundation from September 2016

Lin-Manuel Miranda became famous because of his writing, and he's used that fame to talk about important issues and help other people.

WHERE IT ALL STARTED

Lin-Manuel Miranda had a love for music and theater from a young age. He was born on January 16, 1980, in New York City. His parents—Luz Towns-Miranda and Luis A. Miranda Jr.—are from Puerto Rico. They raised Lin-Manuel and his sister Luz in a proud **Hispanic** neighborhood in New York.

Lin-Manuel listened to all kinds of music while growing up— from hip-hop to Broadway musical cast albums. He also acted in school plays at Hunter College High School. Lin-Manuel knew he wanted to be part of the world of movies, music, and theater. He just had to figure out how to get there.

In His Words

"I was a kid who was always making stuff. I didn't know whether I wanted to make action movies or **animated** cartoons or musicals, but I was always just making stuff."

— Interview with the *Los Angeles Times* from November 2016

Lin-Manuel is still very close with his parents. He's said they've taught him to work hard and to be proud of where he comes from.

WRITING ABOUT HIS WORLD

Lin-Manuel's path to becoming a Broadway writer led him to Wesleyan University—a school where he studied theater. While he was there, he wrote his first draft of *In the Heights*. This musical, which is set in the Washington Heights neighborhood of New York City, is about Latinx people—people from Latin American backgrounds.

Lin-Manuel wanted to create a musical about people like him and his family. When *In the Heights* became a success on Broadway in 2008, it inspired many people. It **represented** the Latinx community in a positive way on stage. Nothing like it had ever been seen on Broadway before!

In His Words

"The success of *In the Heights* gave me a life as a writer, a career as a writer, it said, 'You belong here.' Nothing will ever do for me what that show did—from broke to not broke—in every respect."

— Interview with *Grantland* from September 2015

8

In the Heights won four Tony Awards—the most famous prizes a Broadway show can win. Lin-Manuel wrote the musical with Quiara Alegría Hudes, and he also starred in it as the character Usnavi.

SOMETHING NEW

The idea for Lin-Manuel's next musical came to him while he was on vacation in 2008. He was reading a book about the life of Alexander Hamilton—one of America's Founding Fathers—and decided that he could tell Hamilton's story through hip-hop music.

It took many years, but this idea eventually led Lin-Manuel to write the Broadway musical *Hamilton*. The musical's hip-hop sound wasn't the only groundbreaking thing about it. Lin-Manuel and his fellow creators cast people of color to play the Founding Fathers, who were all white men in real life. This allowed people of all races to see themselves represented in this story.

In His Words

"This is a story about America then, told by America now, and we want to **eliminate** any distance—our story should look the way our country looks … I think it's a very powerful statement without having to be a statement."

— Interview with the *New York Times* about *Hamilton* from February 2015

Lin-Manuel didn't just write *Hamilton*—he also played Alexander Hamilton in the musical!

HAMILTON BECOMES A HIT

In 2015, *Hamilton* began its run on Broadway. It became a huge hit and brought people to Broadway who'd never seen a musical before. *Hamilton* was popular with people of all ages, races, and backgrounds. It got them excited about history, and it helped them see the Founding Fathers as real people.

Hamilton's success led to many awards, including 11 Tony Awards in 2016. The day Hamilton won its Tony Awards, there was a deadly shooting at an **LGBT+** club in Florida. Lin-Manuel used one of his speeches at the Tony Awards to honor the people killed in that shooting.

In His Words

"This show is proof that history remembers
We lived through times when hate and fear seemed stronger;
We rise and fall and light from dying **embers**, remembrances that hope and love last longer
And love is love is love is love is love is love is love is love cannot be killed or swept aside."

— 2016 Tony Awards speech

In 2015, Lin-Manuel helped start the Hamilton Education Program, which brings kids from public schools to see *Hamilton* and helps schools across the country use *Hamilton* to teach young people about history.

IN THE EYE OF A HURRICANE

Lin-Manuel's family is from Puerto Rico, which was hit by Hurricane Maria in 2017. Millions of people on the island lost power, and many people lost their lives. Lin-Manuel knew he wanted to help in whatever ways he could. He started by writing a song.

Lin-Manuel wrote the song "Almost Like Praying," and money from sales of the song went to help people in Puerto Rico. Lin-Manuel got many famous artists, including Jennifer Lopez and Camila Cabello, to sing the song with him. He also brought *Hamilton* to Puerto Rico in 2019 to raise money for the arts on the island.

In His Words

"There's no shortage of ways to do good, and this is just one of them … Music travels faster than news. Music travels faster than anything. And if you can thread the needle and do it right, it lasts longer, too."

– Interview with *TIME* magazine from October 2017

Lin-Manuel did many things to help Puerto Rico **recover** from Hurricane Maria. He raised money and awareness, and he visited the island to deliver food and supplies to the people living there.

USING TWITTER FOR GOOD

Lin-Manuel is also known for his writing on social media. He uses Twitter to share funny stories, to talk about issues that matter to him, and to connect with others.

Lin-Manuel's most well-known writing on Twitter is his collection of "Gmorning" and "Gnight" tweets. During times when he's active on social media, he often shares these tweets every day. They inspire people with their messages of hope, comfort, and kindness. In 2018, his tweets were collected in a book called *Gmorning, Gnight!: Little Pep Talks for Me & You*. The book, which also has art by Jonny Sun, became very popular.

In His Words

"Gmorning.
Try & face the world with your best self, even if the world doesn't **respond** in kind.
Don't do them, do you."

— Tweet from September 2016

Lin-Manuel often uses social media to share stories about his family, including his wife Vanessa and their sons Sebastian and Francisco.

17

STAYING BUSY

After Lin-Manuel stopped playing Alexander Hamilton on Broadway, he found many new ways to stay busy. He's acted in movies such as *Mary Poppins Returns* and on TV shows such as *Brooklyn Nine-Nine* and *His Dark Materials*. His voice has also been used on the animated TV show *DuckTales*.

Lin-Manuel has continued to write too. He wrote music for two *Star Wars* movies and the Disney animated movie *Moana*. Lin-Manuel has also helped bring *In the Heights* to the big screen. He plays the part of Piragua Guy in the movie based on his first hit musical.

In His Words

"I'm the story guy. I'm the one who writes songs that tell stories."

— Interview with the *Los Angeles Times* from November 2016

The Life of Lin-Manuel Miranda

1980
Lin-Manuel Miranda is born on January 16.

2002
Lin-Manuel finishes school at Wesleyan University.

2008
In the Heights starts its run on Broadway and wins 4 Tony Awards.

Lin-Manuel reads the book that inspires him to write *Hamilton*.

2010
Lin-Manuel marries Vanessa Nadal.

2015
Hamilton opens on Broadway.

2016
Hamilton wins 11 Tony Awards.

Lin-Manuel plays Alexander Hamilton for the last time on Broadway.

Moana opens in movie theaters with music by Lin-Manuel.

2017
Lin-Manuel writes "Almost Like Praying" to raise money for Puerto Rico after Hurricane Maria.

2018
Lin-Manuel's tweets become a book called *Gmorning, Gnight!*

Lin-Manuel stars in *Mary Poppins Returns*.

2019
Lin-Manuel brings *Hamilton* to Puerto Rico.

2020
In the Heights opens in movie theaters with Lin-Manuel playing Piragua Guy.

Lin-Manuel Miranda has done many great things in his life so far, and he's sure to do many more!

WORDS CAN CHANGE THE WORLD!

Another example of how Lin-Manuel has used his talents to help others came in March 2018. After a shooting at a high school in Parkland, Florida, students planned a **protest** called the March for Our Lives. Lin-Manuel then recorded a song with fellow Broadway star Ben Platt called "Found/Tonight." It used parts of Lin-Manuel's song "The Story of Tonight" from *Hamilton*. The song raised money for the march, and they sang it at the event.

Lin-Manuel Miranda has found many ways to make a difference as a writer. Whether it's tweets, songs, or entire Broadway musicals, his words are changing the world!

In His Words

"We have this amount of time, it's the tiniest grain of sand of time we're allowed on this Earth to be alive. And what do we leave behind and how much—and we're not even promised a day."

— Interview with *TIME* magazine from April 2016

Be Like
Lin-Manuel Miranda!

Write stories about people who aren't often in the spotlight.

Write about issues that matter to you. You can even write to government leaders!

Make everyone feel included.

If you know someone who's sad, write them a card or letter to show you care about them.

Read all kinds of books and listen to all kinds of music to learn different people's stories.

Use social media to build people up and not to tear them down.

Lin-Manuel Miranda has made a difference as a writer, and so can you! These are just some ways you can start making the world around you a better and brighter place for everyone.

GLOSSARY

animated: Created through a series of drawings or pictures.

eliminate: To put an end to or get rid of.

ember: A glowing piece of coal or wood in the ashes of a fire.

Hispanic: Relating to people from an area where Spanish is spoken, especially Latin America.

inspire: To move someone to do something great.

LGBT+: Relating to a group made up of people who see themselves as a gender different from the sex they were assigned at birth or who want to be in romantic relationships that aren't only male-female. LGBT stands for lesbian, gay, bisexual, and transgender.

musical: A movie or play that tells a story with songs and often dancing.

protest: An event in which people gather to show they do not like something.

recover: To get back to the way things were before.

represent: To show something or someone in a work of art.

respond: To do something as a reaction to something that has happened.

responsibility: A duty that a person should do.

social media: A collection of websites and applications, or apps, that allow users to interact with each other and create online communities.

FOR MORE INFORMATION

WEBSITES

IMDb: Lin-Manuel Miranda

www.imdb.com/name/nm0592135

The Internet Movie Database has a list of all of Lin-Manuel Miranda's past, present, and future projects, as well as facts about his life.

PBS: *Hamilton's America*

www.pbs.org/wnet/gperf/episodes/hamiltons-america

This part of the PBS website features links and videos related to the *Great Performances* episode about *Hamilton*.

BOOKS

Morlock, Theresa. *Lin-Manuel Miranda: Award-Winning Actor, Rapper, Writer, and Composer*. New York, NY: PowerKids Press, 2018.

Nelson, Penelope S. *Lin-Manuel Miranda*. North Mankato, MN: Capstone Press, 2019.

Spanier, Kristine. *Lin-Manuel Miranda*. Minneapolis, MN: Bullfrog Books, 2019.

INDEX